Dinah Wilson Goff

Divine Protection through Extraordinary Dangers during the

Irish Rebellion in 1798

.

Dinah Wilson Goff

Divine Protection through Extraordinary Dangers during the Irish Rebellion in 1798

ISBN/EAN: 9783337124175

Printed in Europe, USA, Canada, Australia, Japan

Cover: Foto ©ninafisch / pixelio.de

More available books at **www.hansebooks.com**

DIVINE PROTECTION

THROUGH

EXTRAORDINARY DANGERS,

DURING THE

IRISH REBELLION IN 1798.

———◆———

PHILADELPHIA:

PUBLISHED BY THE TRACT ASSOCIATION OF FRIENDS,
AND TO BE HAD AT THEIR DEPOSITORY,
NO. 304 ARCH STREET.

DIVINE PROTECTION.

THE Saviour of men frequently inculcated on his followers the duty of avoiding an over-anxious and distrustful disposition, and of confiding in the protecting and preserving care of our Heavenly Father. "Are not five sparrows sold for two farthings," said he, "and not one of them is forgotten before God,"—"one of them shall not fall on the ground without your Father. But the very hairs of your head are all numbered. Fear ye not, therefore, ye are of more value than many sparrows."

It would be difficult to find language to convey in a more touching or striking manner the minuteness of that watchful care which a beneficient Providence is continually exercising over his children even in their temporal affairs; and we believe that a firm belief in the doctrine, and a humble and reverent sense of its importance duly impressed on

the mind, would not only act as an incitement to
watchfulness unto prayer, but greatly mitigate the
sorrows and trials of life. Those who cordially
embrace the belief and daily live in it, will be led
to renounce a dependence on their own skill and
wisdom for the direction of their steps through life,
and earnestly to seek and wait for the guidance of
the Holy Spirit, which leadeth into all truth and
out of every evil way.

Many are the instances in which those thus engaged have experienced the happy effects of following the unfoldings of the Divine Light even in
very small things; when, if they had pursued the
course which worldly wisdom had dictated, the
consequences would have been afflicting. Our
vision is very limited and imperfect, and our
judgments of men and things exceedingly liable
to error; and while it becomes such a frail and
unworthy creature as man to speak cautiously and
with deep humility of divine direction, it is none
the less his duty to be daily striving for it, in
abasedness of soul, as an unspeakable and unmerited favor, vouchsafed, in great condescension,
to the sincere seeker.

The following narrative, written by Dinah W.
Goff, gives some account of the dangers and trials
to which her parents, Jacob and Elizabeth Goff,
and their family, were subjected during the fear-

ful scenes of the Irish Rebellion, in 1798. These Friends, relying on the gracious, protecting care of the Almighty for deliverance from lawless men, refused either to take up arms in their own defence, or to quit the perilous post of duty. The christian disposition of meekness and forbearance, strengthened by a holy courage and firmness, proved in this instance, as in many others, the means, under the divine blessing, of safety amid circumstances of extraordinary trial. On the other hand, the declaration of our Lord and Saviour is often fulfilled, that they who take the sword shall perish by it. The wrathful and violent, whether individuals or nations, frequently bring destruction on themselves, while the gentle and inoffensive dwell in security and peace.

The account commences thus, viz :—

It has often occurred to me that I ought to leave some little memorial of the preservation extended by our Heavenly Father to my beloved parents and the family, as well as of the remarkable faith and patience with which they were favored, under circumstances of a very peculiar and distressing character.

It was about the middle of the Fifth month, 1798, that the county of Wexford, in Ireland, became a scene of open rebellion, headed by B—— H——, a Protestant, and two Roman Ca-

1*

tholic Priests, John Murphy and Philip Roche.* The aims of the insurgents were various; some were more cruelly disposed than others; all determined to liberate themselves by force of arms from the unequal yoke, as they believed it, of the British government, and to become a free people; some to bring all Ireland to Catholicism, &c.

" About ten days before the rebellion broke out, a Roman Catholic, who resided near, called on my father, and desired to speak to him in private. He then informed him that the county would, in the course of a few days, be in a state of general insurrection. My father replied that he could not credit it, for that he had frequently heard such rumors. The person assured him that he knew certainly it would be so, and that he had procured a vessel, now lying at Duncannon, to convey himself and family to Wales; and that, as a friend, he gladly offered accommodation to our household. My father thanked him for this act of friendship, but said that it felt to him a matter of great importance to remove from the position allotted him by Providence, yet that he would consider of it, and consult his wife. After having endeavored to seek

* Murphy was chief instigator to cruelty and murder; he pretended to catch the flying bullets of the royalist troops, but was at length killed by a cannon ball. Roche, though more humane, was finally hung.

best wisdom, my dear parents concluded that it was right for them to remain at home, placing their dependence and confidence in Him who alone can protect, and who has promised to preserve those that put their trust in him.

The estate and spacious mansion, called Horetown, occupied by my parents, Jacob and Elizabeth Goff, and the family, were situated about ten miles from each of the towns of Wexford and New Ross. The rebels formed two camps, at Carrickburn and Corbitt Hill, one on each side of the house, at distances of two and five miles from it. This central position caused a constant demand on us for provisions, with which the insurgents were daily supplied, and they often said that they spared the lives of the family for that purpose.

A day or two after the commencement of the rebellion, two carts were brought to our door, and the cellars emptied of all the salt provisions, beer, cider, &c., which were taken off to the camp. Fourteen beautiful horses were turned out of my father's stables, and mounted in the yard by two or more of the rebels on each. Some, which had not been trained, resisted by plunging; but their riders soon subdued them, running their pikes into them, and otherwise using great cruelty. Much of our cattle they also took off, and orders were sent each week from the camp at Carrickburn, to have a cow and some sheep killed, which were sent for at stated times.

Soon after the general rising and arming of the people in the county of Wexford,* we were roused one morning by the sound of cannon at a distance, and quickly heard that there had been an engagement at a place called "The Three Rocks," on the mountains of Forth, near Wexford, between the yeomanry and the rebels. After a severe conflict, the former were put to flight, with great loss of life; sixty or seventy were buried in one grave.

Two of my cousins named Heatly, whose mother had married out of our society, were officers in that corps, and escaped to our house under cover of the darkness of night. On their arrival, they found that their father and mother, and seven or eight children had been turned out of their comfortable home, and had also fled for refuge to my father's, where they were affectionately received. We had all retired to rest when these young officers arrived.

---

* Keightley remarks: "It was in the county of Wexford that the rebellion really raged—a county which would probably have remained at rest, had not the people been goaded into rebellion by the cruelties inflicted by the military and the self-styled loyalists. It was here only that priests appeared among the rebels, and that murders on a large scale were perpetrated by them."— *Hist. of England*, vol. iii.

The thankfulness of their parents, who had never expected to see them again, passes all description: they were much affected, and immediately returned thanks, on the bended knee, for the preservation of their children. For some days, the two young men remained in the house, hiding from room to room, sometimes under the beds, as there was a frequent search for arms and Orangemen by the rebels. Some of the chiefs of these, having information of their being with us, called, demanding them to surrender, and offering them the United Irishmen's Oath. This, however, they resolutely refused, saying they had taken the oath of allegiance to their sovereign but a few days before, and would never perjure themselves. On this, one of the rebels laid his hand on his sword, and in great irritation said, " were it not for the respect they had for Mr. Goff, and that they did not wish to spill blood in his hall, their lives should be the forfeit of their refusal." At length, my cousins left our house at night, intending to make their way to Ross, and took shelter in the cottage of an old Roman Catholic nurse employed by the family; but by her they were betrayed, and handed over to the rebels, who took them prisoners to the camp. The lives of these interesting young men were, however, remarkably preserved, after they had endured much hardship in prison.

Two Roman Catholic men-servants, belonging to our family and lodging in the house, were compelled to join the rebels to save their lives; and were armed with pikes—the first we had seen. On my dear mother's hearing of their having brought these weapons, she sent to let them know she could not allow anything of the kind to be brought into her house; so each night they left them outside the door. They behaved quietly and respectfully throughout, generally returning home at the close of the day.

The rebels set fire to the houses of many Protestants; and in the morning after the general rising, a Roman Catholic family, seven in number, came from Enniscorthy, apparently in great distress, saying they left the town on fire. They received shelter and hospitable entertainment from my dear parents, and remained with us the whole time. My mother often remarked, with reference to her large family, that provisions from day to day were so wonderfully granted that it seemed, like the cruise of oil and the barrel of meal, never-failing.

About twenty persons surrounded our dinner table each day, beside those in the kitchen, four of whom were members of our Society; which my mother considered a great advantage at that awful period. She frequently said that "hind's feet" appeared to be given her, in being enabled with extraordinary ease to get through the numerous household duties that then devolved upon her. Thus the gracious promise was verified in her experience:—"As thy days so shall thy strength be."

A rebel once inquired of her, "Madam, do you think we shall gain the day?" Feeling it to be a serious question, after a pause, she replied, "The Almighty only knows." He answered, "You are right, madam; have a good heart; not a *hair* of *your* head shall be hurt; but when this business is over, the Quakers are all to be driven down into Connaught, where the land is worth about two-pence an acre, and you will have to till *that*, and live on it as you can." My mother smiled and said, "Give *us* a good portion, for we have a large family."

Hannah and Arabella (afterwards Fennell), with Dinah W. Goff, aged about thirty, nineteen and fourteen, were the only daughters at home at this time. The former two usually walked three miles on First-days to the meeting-house at Forrest, accompanied by two of the women-servants, though they met with many interruptions on the way.

One day some of the people said, as they passed the Roman Catholic chapel, "How they dare us by going through the streets! If they persist, they shall be taken and dragged to the altar of the chapel, and suffer the penalty of their obstinacy." But my sisters passed quietly on. On one of these occasions, they remarked that a strange dog accompanied them ; it followed them for some miles, and when they got safe home, could not be induced to enter the house, but went away. This circumstance, though simple, seemed remarkable at the time. I fully believe that their minds were not resting on outward help, but on that Omnipotent arm which was mercifully underneath to sustain. They were enabled regularly to pursue their way, and to unite with the few Friends that were permitted to meet, remarking those opportunities as being peculiarly solemn. Our dear parents would gladly have joined them, but were unable, from the infirmities of age, to walk so far, and had no horses left to draw a carriage.

The family were always assembled for the purpose of reading the Scriptures, after the fatigues of the day were over ; and one evening, a priest coming in, as he often did at other times, perhaps to see what we were doing, remarked on the quietude which prevailed. My mother said it was usually the case when the hurry of household cares had ceased. He said he came with good news— that we were now all of one religion the world over. My mother then inquired what it was, as she believed there was only one true religion. He replied, that an edict from the Pope had arrived, and that it proclaimed the universal Roman

Catholic religion, adding that it was high time for her to put up the cross. She asked what he meant by the cross. He said, " Put up the outward sign on yourself and your children." She answered, *That* they should never do; but she was thankful in believing that her heavenly Father was enabling her to bear the cross, and that she trusted He might be pleased to continue to do so to the end. I was standing near him at the time, when he put his arms round me, and said, " My dear child, we shall have you all to ourselves ;" and, placing his hand on my father's shoulder, he said, " Mr. Goff, you shall be one of our head senators." This unhappy man, we afterwards heard, lost his life in attacking a Protestant gentleman, on whose kindness and hospitality he had thrown himself, when his own house was burnt down by the English troops. To us he was uniformly kind, and we thought his attention might, under Providence, have had some influence on the minds of the rebels.

Many hundreds were daily on our lawn, and our business was to hand them food as they demanded it. Their fatigue and the heat of summer being exhausting, large tubs of milk and water were placed at the hall and back doors, with great quantities of bread and cheese. The servants were frequently obliged to stay up all night to bake bread for them, and my mother and sisters often

2

made their hands bleed in cutting the bread and cheese: if not cut up, they would carry off whole loaves and cheeses at the ends of their pikes. They took carving-knives and others of large size from the pantry to fasten on poles, thus converting them into destructive weapons: on seeing which, my mother had the remainder carefully locked up after the meals. At times, they gave us dreadful details of their own cruelty, and of the agonies of the sufferers, to the great distress of my sisters and myself. One day after a battle, they related many such acts. I was handing them food at the time, and could not refrain from bursting into tears, throwing down what I had in my hand, and running away into the house.

We were greatly struck by observing that, however outrageously a party might come, there were generally some among them who were disposed to promote peace. Such would say, "You ought not to treat them so—the poor ladies who have been up all night making bread for you with their own hands." One morning a most violent party advanced, yelling and swearing hideously, like savages intent on rapine, so that we fully believed they had formed some wicked design; but two young men, who looked sorrowful and alarmed on our behalf, though perfect strangers, came forward, requesting we might all withdraw and shut the door, as they could not but dread the consequences if the party were allowed to enter the house. The young men stationed themselves on the steps of the hall-door, drew their great cavalry swords, and, flourishing them, declared that no one should pass; pleading for us in the most kind and energetic manner—" Why would you injure Mr. Goff and his family, who are doing all they can, feeding and providing for you ?" After a long struggle, the company relinquished their evil purpose. The young men were quite overcome with the exertion and heat: my father warmly thanked them, and gave them silk handkerchiefs to wipe their faces, inquiring their names—one of them was called Dennis —— of Gorey. On that occasion, many wicked-looking women were outside, evidently waiting for plunder; and, when disappointed, they made frightful faces, and shook their hands at us as we stood at the windows. One of them was heard to say when they withdrew, " You are a set of chicken-hearted fellows !"

A severe conflict took place at Enniscorthy, the garrison being forced to surrender, and many hundreds, as we were told, left dead in the streets. Two days after it, our Quarterly Meeting for Leinster province was, in usual course, held there; and was attended by David Sands from America, a valued minister of our Society, who was then traveling through Ireland, with Abraham Jackson as his companion. As they passed through Enniscorthy, the latter had to alight and assist in removing the dead bodies, which still lay in the streets, from before the wheels of the carriage. The meeting, though small, was said to have been remarkably solemn, as it well might be, and also much favored : many other Friends with ourselves were deprived of the means of attending, by the want of horses which the rebels had taken.

A barn, about a mile and a half from us, belonging to a gentleman who lived at Scullabogue, was used as a prison, in which about two hundred and fifty persons, chiefly Protestants, were confined —men, women, and children, some being infants in their mothers' arms. There they remained from Sixth until Third-day, without receiving any food, except some sheaves of wheat occasionally thrown in, that the rebels might have the amusement of seeing them scramble for the grains. On the day of the battle of New Ross, sixty or more of them were brought out on the lawn, and offered, one by one, life and liberty if they would change their religious profession ; but they all refused. Some, after being half tortured to death, answered, " No ; give me more powder and ball first."

[The cases of two prisoners, who were brothers, named John and Samuel Jones, are particularly touching. On their refusal to turn Catholics, they were offered their lives if they would say that they were Friends. This they did not feel at liberty to do, not being in membership, although Friends in principle. John was first executed, while Samuel, who was kindly supported by his wife, quoted the text, "He that loseth his life for my sake, shall find it." He bore his martyrdom with firmness, and was put to death after being shot at five times.] The wife, with admirable fortitude stood between them when they were shot, and held up a hand of each. She then implored the murderers to take her life also; but they refused, saying, "They would not dishonor the Virgin Mary by killing a woman." I saw her afterwards in deep affliction passing our gate, as she sat in a cart with the remains of her husband and brother. On the same day,—viz. the 4th of Sixth month,—the barn was set on fire, and all the other prisoners (said to be one hundred and eighty-four) were consumed. Some of the poor women put their infants out through the windows, hoping to save them; but the ruffians took them up on their pikes, and threw them back into the flames. I saw the smoke of the barn, and cannot now forget the strong and dreadful effluvium which was wafted from it to our lawn.*

* Yet Keightley remarks—"We fear, if a fair balance

2*

In the engagement at New Ross the insurgents
were defeated. This was an awful scene of conflict
and bloodshed, continuing with but little cessation
for nearly twelve hours. It is stated that two
thousand persons were killed. The king's troops
retreated twice, and the town was in the hands of
the rebels, when a reinforcement was understood to
have come up and put them to flight. Some
asserted that no reinforcement arrived, and that the
assailing multitude fled when there were none to
pursue them. General Johnson, who commanded
the royalists, said that the success of that day was
to be attributed to Providence, and was not the
work of man. Several Friends of New Ross had
previously retired to Waterford; others who
remained were remarkably preserved, though the
town was set on fire in different quarters.

Previously to the burning of the barn, a company
came one day with two horses, saying they had
orders to take my dear father and our cousin,
J. Heatly, to the camp—the latter being the father
of the two young officers before-mentioned. It was
nearly noon when they came and seized their two
victims ; and my mother having gone to give some

were struck of the bloodshed, the cruelties, and the other
enormities committed during these unhappy times, that
the preponderance would be greatly on the side of the
royalists.''

orders in the kitchen, I ran to call her, saying they were forcing my father on horseback. On this she came out, and pressing through the dense crowd on the lawn, asked them peremptorily, " What are you doing with my husband?" On their saying they were going to take him to the camp, she said, in the same tone, " You shall not take my husband, for he is in poor health; and if you put him in prison, I think he could not live many weeks: he will be here for you at any time you wish, as he cannot leave his house." They were then silent, and quietly relinquished their design. My mother remarked, " We have got what you call protections from the generals." These were sent for, and read aloud, to this effect:—" Let no one molest Mr. Goff or his family, they being hostages to the united army. Signed in the camp of Carrickburn by two generals, Harvey and Roche." These documents had been previously sent without any request made by the family. The party were then satisfied, as related to my father: all entreaty was, however, unavailing with respect to my cousin, J. Heatly, who was taken away on horseback, amid the shrieks and cries of his afflicted wife and children.

We afterwards heard that they soon made him dismount, and walk ten miles to Wexford. They then put him on board a prison-ship on the river Slaney, where he remained until the insurgents were totally defeated. He witnessed many of his acquaintances and fellow-sufferers—said to be to the number of ninety-seven in all—taken out of the same ship and put to death, with very cruel circumstances, on the Wexford Bridge; but he and a friend of his had a remarkable escape. The prisoners were called out by two and two; and when it came to his and his friend's turn, he made some excuses for delay. The rebels continued calling for them from the deck of the vessel, with their bayonets pointed down towards them; but they still delayed going. At this juncture, a rumor reached their guards that the English army were marching into the town; and this report throwing them into a state of terror, the lives of the two prisoners were saved. It proved, however, to be only a few yeomen, boldly preceded by an officer of the corps, which had been defeated in the engagement on the mountains of Forth. The rebels took flight in all directions, and Wexford was left in possession of the English, to the great joy of the loyal inhabitants, who had suffered many privations and cruelties.

John Heatly often related the circumstance afterwards, saying that Providence had in an extraordinary manner saved his life. He had been many years in the navy. His house, Rock View, was occupied for some time by the rebels, who left it a complete wreck.

A party, who assumed the rank of officers in the rebel army, came to our house one day, and directed to have dinner prepared immediately. On my mother's requesting the servant to lay the tables in the hall, they indignantly asked, "Is it there you are going to give us our dinner? Show us into the best parlor in the house." But on my mother assuring them that she had seen noblemen sitting in that hall, they became calm and satisfied. They then asked for spirits and wine, saying they would have some; and when my mother told them that there were none in the house, they were greatly irritated, still saying they must have some. On being spoken to by my mother in the singular number, they desired her not to say thee and thou to them, as if she were speaking to a dog; and on her again saying "thou" to one of them, he flourished his sword over her head, and said, haughtily, "No more of your theeing and thouing to me." They ate their dinner, however, and went off peaceably.

We were now informed that orders had been given to take my dear father's life, and my mother was most particular in keeping us all close together around him, saying that if it were permitted that our lives should be taken, we might be enabled to support and encourage each other, or else all go together! One day, about noon, a large company

appeared on the lawn, carrying a black flag, which
we well knew to be the signal for death. My dear
father advanced to meet them as usual, with his
open, benevolent countenance. and my mother,
turning to me, said, with her sweet, placid smile,
"Perhaps my stiff stays may prevent my dying
easily." On which the Roman Catholic who had
taken refuge with us, said, "Have faith in God,
madam; I hope they will not hurt *you:*" she
quickly pushed forward and joined my dear father.
who was surrounded by a large party. He
observed to them, he feared they might injure each
other, as their muskets were prepared for firing;
when one of them replied. "Let those who are
afraid keep out of the way." My mother distinctly
heard one of them say, "Why don't you begin?"
and each seemed looking to the other to commence
the work of death. Some of them presently mut-
tered, "We cannot." At this critical moment, some
women came in great agitation through the crowd,
clinging to their husbands, and dragging them
away. Thus a higher Power evidently appeared
to frustrate the intentions of the murderers, and
my beloved father was again graciously delivered.
One man said there was "no use in taking Mr.
Goff's life;" but his two sons, if there, should soon
be killed, and then the estate would be theirs.

One morning a most outrageous party advanced

towards the house, yelling and roaring like savages, evidently with some wicked design; but two young men who looked serious again interposed in our behalf, and would not allow them to enter. Thus were the words of David fulfilled: "The wrath of man shall praise thee; the remainder of wrath thou wilt restrain."

A young man, who, with his mother, kept a neighboring public house, used at that time often to walk into our drawing-room, lay his sword on the table, and amuse me and my young cousin by giving us his finely decorated hat to admire. One afternoon he tried to prevail on us two to go with him to the camp, saying it was an interesting sight, such as we might never have an opportunity again to see. We were then sixteen and fourteen years of age; and on my saying I did not think my mother would permit us to go, he desired us not to tell her, and promised to bring us safely back. My mother, ever watchful, was at this moment crossing the hall; and seeing us together, she came forward and inquired what he was saying. When we told her, she asked him how he dared to request the children to go to such a place? She then reasoned with us on the impropriety of listening to such invitations, saying she should never have expected to see us again if we had once gone.

Three or four hundred English troops, accompanied by Hompesch's German hussars, at length landed at Duncannon Fort; this was announced by the firing of cannon early in the morning. On my mother's entering my room, I expressed much pleasure at the intelligence, when she replied: "My dear, we must rejoice with trembling; having much to dread from their being strangers, and we know not what may be permitted; we have only to place our trust and confidence in Him who hath hitherto preserved us!" This little army formed an encampment on my late uncle Cæsar Sutton's lawn at Longgrague, about two miles from us. The next day, whilst we were sitting at dinner, one of the servants said the rebel forces were coming from Wexford in thousands, intending to surround the English encampment. The royal troops, commanded by General Moore, having had previous information, were, however, on the alert, and met them on the road near our house. We counted twenty-four pieces of cannon belonging to the rebels, which passed our entrance. A dreadful scene, partly in our view, was now enacted, and lasted for three hours. The firing was awful! Having closed the doors and windows in the lower part of the house as much as possible, we all retired to an upper room, and there remained in a state of fearful suspense. It was a terrible sight, and deeply affected us, the cannon balls falling thickly about the house. On one of my sisters raising the window to look out, a ball whizzed by her head; and this, with many others, we afterwards found. At length, seeing the poor, deluded people running in all directions, we learned that they were routed.

Two soon came to the house to have their wounds dressed, which my sister Arabella did as well as she could; one had a ball in the cap of his knee, and both bled profusely. They expressed much thankfulness, and hoped they might soon be able again to fight for their freedom. A fine young man coming, who had received a severe wound in his side and shoulder, my dear mother used means to relieve him, and dressed him comfortably in clean linen, while he frequently exclaimed, "Do, ma'am, try to stop the blood. I don't mind the pain, so that I may but fight for my liberty." Observing him in danger from the great injury, she spoke to him in a very serious strain, and also recommended his going to the Wexford Infirmary. We heard afterwards that he died on the way a few hours after he left us. This battle was at Goff's Bridge, on the 20th of Sixth month. Several hundreds of the insurgents were killed, but not many of the military.

Soon after the firing had ceased, we observed two of the cavalry moving slowly and suspiciously up our avenue; on which my father went down to

3

the hall door, and advanced with a smiling countenance and extended arms to meet them. One, who
was a German, at once embraced him, saying, in
broken English, "You be Friend—no enemy, no
enemy;" and gave him the kiss of peace; adding,
"We have Friends in Germany." We got them
eggs, milk, bread, &c., to refresh them, after the
excessive fatigue and excitement which it was
obvious they had suffered.

The evening before this engagement, one of my
sisters, passing through the servants' hall, observed
the coachman leaning on his arm, apparently much
distressed. When she requested to know the cause,
he hesitated and said he could not tell her; but on
her entreating him, and adding that she should like
to know the worst, he said that he had heard it
planned at the camp, that, if they conquered the
royalists, we were all to be murdered, and the generals were to take possession of our house. He then
added, weeping, "Oh, our plans are too wicked for
the Lord to prosper them!" My sister remarked
that we trusted in a Power stronger than man, and
able to protect us in the midst of danger; or to
that effect

During the night following this battle, our house
was surrounded by Hompesch's cavalry, who slept
on the lawn wrapped up in their grey coats. The
next morning twenty or thirty of the officers break-

fasted with us, and told us that we had had a mar-
vellous escape on the previous day; the cannon
having been placed on the bridge, and pointed
against the house to batter it down; even the
match was lighted, when a gentleman, who knew
my father and us, came forward, and told them the
house was "inhabited by a loyal Quaker and his
family." They had previously supposed it must
be a rendezvous of rebels, and feared, from its
commanding position, that they themselves might
have been fired upon from it. Some of the officers, being refreshed by their meal, even shed
tears when they reflected on the danger we had
been in.

My cousins, Richard and Ann Goff, of Hope-
field, near Horetown, had been observed by "the
United Men" to persevere in walking to Forrest
Meeting, whilst the country was in a state of rebellion; and were apprised that, if they continued
this practice, and refused to unite in the Roman
Catholic forms of worship, they should be put to
death, and their house burned. This threat brought
them under deep mental exercise, accompanied with
fervent prayers that they might be enabled to come
to a right decision; and, collecting their large family
together, in humble confidence that best direction
might be mercifully afforded, after a season of
solemn retirement, they laid the matter before their

children. On this memorable occasion, the noble
and intrepid language of Fade Goff, their eldest
son, then about seventeen years of age, is worthy
of being recorded. "Father," said he, "rejoice
that we are found worthy to suffer." His parents
were deeply affected, and their minds became so
much strengthened, that next morning, rising before
daybreak, they all proceeded to the meeting, and
were enabled to continue to attend Divine worship
without molestation; expressing thankfulness in
thus being permitted to accomplish what they considered their religious duty.

David Sands and his companion attended that
meeting, and, returning to Horetown, were joyfully
received by us: my dear mother saying that his
visit reminded her of the good Samaritan pouring
oil into our wounded minds. The three families
now occupying our house all assembled with him
on this solemn occasion, and his communication
was truly impressive and consoling, inducing ten-
derness in all present. He first alluded to the deep
trials we had suffered; then to the infinite mercy
which had brought the family through them; and
afterwards offered a solemn tribute of thanksgiving
and praise to the great Preserver of men, whose
power had been so remarkably displayed for our
protection, when surrounded by danger on every
hand. It was, indeed, a memorable visit, for which

thankfulness prevailed to Him from whom all con-
solation is derived. The Roman Catholic family
had never before heard these plain truths so
declared, nor witnessed anything of the kind; but
they all united in prayer on their knees, and the
mother said : " I never heard such a minister as
that gentleman ; he must be an angel from Heaven
sent to you!"

The rebellion was now at an end; but, though
peace and order were partially restored to our
afflicted country, yet the sad consequences still remained ; not only houses in ruins, burned and torn
in pieces by both armies, were to be seen in all
directions, but many of the rebels who were out-
lawed, took up their abode in caverns in the wood
of Killoughran, and sallied forth by night to com-
mit depredations on such of the peaceable inhabitants as had returned to their dilapidated dwellings.
Twice they visited us, and on these occasions our
sufferings were greater than on any during the
rebellion. My father had been urged to accept the
nightly services of a guard of yeomanry, but always positively refused.

On the first night, having all retired to rest, we
were aroused by a terrific knocking with muskets
at the hall door. My dear father raised his chamber window, and requested them to wait a few
minutes, and he would open the door ; but they con-
3*

tinued knocking still louder, and swearing most
awfully until he went down. On his opening the
door, they seized him, and instantly rushed up to
his room, breaking a mahogany desk and book-
case to pieces with their muskets, and demanding
money. My father handed them twenty guineas,
which was all he had in the house ; but they per-
sisted in asking for more, and swore, in a most
profane manner, that if he did not give them more,
they would take his life. I slept with a little niece
in a room inside his, and we were entreated by my
sister A. not to rise, as we should be of no use. I
endeavored to comply with her request, and remain quiet, till I heard a dreadful scuffle, and my
father's voice exclaiming, " Don't murder me !" I
could then no longer keep still, but opened the
door, and saw one of the men, dressed in scarlet
regimentals, with full uniform, epaulettes, &c.,
rushing towards my father with a drawn sword in
his hand. My sister intercepted it by throwing
her arms around my father's neck, when the point
of the sword touched her side, but not so as to injure
her. In the struggle the candle went out, and
they called most violently for light. The horror
which I felt at this awful moment can scarcely be
expressed. My sister went down towards the
kitchen, and found a man standing at the foot of
the first flight of stairs ; she asked him to light the

candle; when he said she might go down, and he
would stand guard, and not allow any one to pass.
This he performed faithfully, and she returned in
safety. I could not, after this, leave the party, but
followed them through the house. The dreadful
language they used, some of which was addressed
to my sisters, impresses me with horror to this day.
Money seemed the sole object of their visit that
night, as they repeatedly said, "Give me more
money, I tell you;" assuring my father that, if he
did not give them more, they would murder him.
They even said from minute to minute, while they
held a pistol to his forehead, "Now you're just
gone." They then forced him to kneel down, re-
peating the same words, and presenting the pistol.
Seeing his situation, I threw myself on my knees
on the floor, and clung with my arms round him;
when the ruffians pushed me away, saying, "You'll
be killed if you stop there." But my father drew
me towards him more closely, saying, "She would
rather be hurt if I am." They snapped the pistol
several times, which perhaps was not charged, as it
did not go off. When they found there was no
more money, they desisted, asking for watches,
which were given them; and at length they went
away, after eating and drinking all they could obtain, and charging my father to have more money
for them the next time, or they declared they would

have his life. So saying, one of them, who appeared in a great rage, and had a cavalry sword in his hand, cut at the handrail of the hall stairs, the mark of which still remains.

About a fortnight afterwards, before the family withdrew to rest, my father had a presentiment that the robbers might come again that night, and sat up later than usual. About midnight they arrived, knocking furiously as before, and fully prepared to plunder the house. They soon emptied the drawers, and took all the wearing apparel they could get, that did not betray the costume of Friends; so that we were deprived of nearly all our clothes. On perceiving that they were taking all, my mother begged one shirt and one pair of stockings for my father, which they threw at her face in the rudest manner, using dreadful language. They behaved most violently, and, spreading quilts and sheets on the floor, filled them with all sorts of clothing they could get; they then called for victuals to eat and drink, desiring my sister to drink their health, putting the cup of small beer to her lips, and bidding her "wish long life and success to the babes of the wood," as they called themselves. This she steadfastly refused. They then declared they would come again in two weeks, and take us all to live with them in the wood, "and to cut bread and butter for the babes." Their behavior was so insulting, and my dear parents were so fearful of these threats being realized, that they determined on sending us young females to my cousins Goff and Neville, who were then merchants in Ross; and there we remained for some weeks, until tranquillity was restored to the country.

After the robbers had finished their repast, they threatened to take my father's life, behaving very outrageously, and saying they must take him to their main guard at a little distance, and murder him there, as they did not like to do it in his own house. They then led him out, and we all attempted to follow; but they pushed my mother back, saying that she should not come—it would be too painful a sight for her to see her husband murdered, which they certainly would do. It was very dark, but my sister Arabella positively refused to leave her father, and they allowed her to accompany him. Whilst crossing the lawn, the root of a beech-tree, projecting above the path, caused him to stumble; he then sat down, and said, if they were determined to take his life, they might as well do it there. My dear sister stood by in a state of awful suspense. They rudely asked him if he had anything to say, telling him his time was come. On hearing this, he remained quite silent, and they, not understanding it, hurried him to speak; when he said, he prayed that the Al-

mighty might be merciful to him, and be pleased
to forgive him his trespasses and sins, and also to
forgive *them*, as *he* did sincerely. They said that
was a good wish, and inquired if he had anything
more to say. He requested them to be tender towards his wife and children; on which they said,
"Good night, Mr. Goff; we only wanted to rattle
the mocuses out of you,"—meaning guineas.

When they took my father forcibly out of the
house, my mother, though much distressed, was
favored with her usual quietude and composure
of mind, trusting in the Lord, who had been
pleased to support her through many deep trials,
and then forsook her not. So strong was her confidence, that she even called to the servant for
some warm water, to prepare a little negus for my
dear father against his return; when I said, "It is
not likely we shall ever see my father again alive,
for they are going to murder him:" on which she
replied, with firmness: "I have faith to believe
they will never be permitted to take his life." In
about a quarter of an hour, my valued and tender
parent returned, pale and exhausted; and throwing himself on the sofa, said : "This work will finish
me; I cannot hold out much longer:" which
proved to be the case.

Remarkable also was the protecting care vouchsafed to my uncle Joshua Wilson (my mother's

brother,) whose residence at Mount Prospect, near
Rathangan, was forcibly entered by a party of
rebels. One night, after the family had retired to
rest, they were aroused by a tremendous volley of
musketry, which at once shattered the hall door;
and a loud cry was raised, of "Arms, money, or
life!" with most awful swearing. My uncle went
hastily down in his dressing-gown, followed by his
wife, who heard them exclaim: "You are a dead
man!" and seeing one of the men present a pistol
at my uncle's head, she rushed between him and
the ruffian, exclaiming: "Thou shalt not, and
darest not, take my husband's life, or touch him;
for the arm of the Almighty is stronger than thou
art!" The man appeared confounded, and let the
pistol drop from his powerless hand; it was very
remarkable, that the whole party left the house soon
after, without doing any further injury.

Many were the heart-rending sufferings that
some families endured, being turned out of their
peaceful homes, and spending many nights in the
fields and ditches. Others, who still remained in
their houses, were wonderfully favored with faith
and patience under great privations, conscientiously
adhering to the revealed law of their God, and thus
experiencing, to their humbling admiration, the
name of the Lord to be "a strong tower," in which
the righteous find safety. On taking a retrospect

of this awful period, and of the strength of mind
evinced by my beloved parents, sisters, and others,
my heart overflows with living praise and thanksgiving to the Father of mercies, and God of all con-
solation, who was, indeed, "strength in weakness,
riches in poverty, and a very present helper in the
time of need."

The repeated shocks and trials, which my hon-
ored father endured during these fearful times,
were too great for his strength of body; and on
the 23d of Twelfth month, in the same year, 1798,
surrounded by many of his family, he gently and
peacefully breathed his last, being then in his sixty-
third year. Our merciful Saviour sweetly sustained him in faith and confidence; his almighty
arm being underneath to comfort and support him
whilst passing through the valley of the shadow of
death. He never expressed a murmur; but, in
humble Christian patience and acquiescence with
the Divine will, often evinced his thankfulness for
the mercies received. To one of my sisters, whom
he observed weeping a short time before his death,
he said: "Do not shed a tear for me, my dear;
but rather rejoice and be thankful that the Almighty has been pleased to permit me to die in
peace, with my dear family around me; and not
by the hands of wicked and unreasonable men."
He took my hand affectionately, and said: "My

dear child, I must leave you all;" and, after a pause, added: "Keep near to the Lord, and he will be a Father and a Friend to thee, when I am no more."

Horetown now passed to my eldest brother, William Goff, and my beloved mother removed to Dublin. She survived her affectionate husband nineteen years, and died in that city in the seventy-eighth year of her age, in perfect peace. For several years she was in the station of an elder. She always endeavored to rule her own house well, and was accounted worthy of double honor, and much beloved by her many descendants. Sixty children, grandchildren and great-grandchildren, were living at the period of her decease, in the year 1817.

She was granddaughter of Thomas Wilson, an account of whose religious labors is published with James Dickinson's. Her last illness was short, being caused by a paralytic seizure, of which she had previously had several. On the morning before the seizure, she entered the drawing-room with an expression of countenance remarkably solemn, and, kneeling down at my side, engaged in fervent vocal supplication for her numerous family, that the blessing of the Most High might rest on them, and that He might be pleased to continue with her to the end. Many consoling expressions she uttered, and when near the close, she said to me: "May the

4*

blessing of the everlasting hills surround thee, my dear child, when I am gone." She was perfectly conscious to the last, and sweetly resigned to her divine Master's will.

It is comforting to have a well-grounded hope, that, through the mediation and redeeming love of our blessed Saviour, the spirits of both my beloved parents have entered into the mansions prepared for the faithful; and that they are, through unmerited mercy, united to the just of all generations, " who have washed their robes, and made them white in the blood of the Lamb;" to whom be glory and honor, for ever and ever!

Thus have I cause to commemorate the great goodness and mercy extended by our heavenly Father to his unworthy creatures throughout a season of inexpressible trial and distress. May his gracious dealings never be forgotten by one who feels undeserving of the least of all his mercies, and who, in taking a retrospective view, can gratefully adopt the language, " Bless the` Lord, O my soul, and forget not all his benefits!"

I am the only one now remaining of twenty-two children, and ever felt much attachment to my parents, whose pious and watchful care over their large family, in our early years, lives in my heart as a sweet memorial, calling for gratitude to Him who gives us pious friends. This feeling, I believe, was cherished by all the rest of their children, now, I humbly trust, through unmerited mercy and redeeming love, united to them in that happy state, where all trials and sorrows are at an end, and where all is joy unspeakable and full of glory.

The foregoing has been written from memory, after a lapse of nearly fifty-nine years, the affecting events being still vivid in my recollection.

DINAH WILSON GOFF.

PENZANCE, Cornwall, 12th mo. 23d, 1856.

A sum of money was raised by government to compensate the sufferers in property, and a portion of it was offered to Jacob Goff, with others, in consideration of the great loss and damage he sustained; but, as a member of the society of Friends, and not taking up arms in defence of government, he felt that he could not accept it.

It is worthy of commemoration and cause of humble thankfulness to the Preserver of men, that amidst the carnage and destruction which frequently prevailed in some parts of Ireland, during this rebellion, and notwithstanding the jeopardy in which some Friends stood every hour, and that they had frequently to pass among violent and enraged men, in going to, and returning from, their religious meetings—which, with very few exceptions, were constantly kept up—the lives of Friends were so

signally preserved, that no member of the society
was put to death, except one young man. That an
exception should be made of one young man, is a
remarkable occurrence; and it is interesting to in-
quire under what circumstances the death of this
individual took place. Sometimes an apparent exception confirms the law; and it will be found that
this very instance is a case of this kind. The
young man alluded to, apprehending that his life
was in danger, and that he could find no means of
defence, took up the resolution accordingly, to put
on a military uniform, and to associate with armed
men. He told his connections that they would all
be murdered, if they remained in such a defenceless
state in the country, and taking with him some
papers of consequence, he fled to a neighboring garrison town. But it so happened, that the very town
he chose as a place of refuge, was attacked and
taken by the insurgents; and, from the most credit-
able information that can be collected, it appears
that when the contest was over, and he was wan-
tonly firing out of a window upon them, the door
of the house was forced open by the enraged enemy;
and, in terror of his life, he sought to conceal himself in an upper chamber, where he was soon dis-
covered and put to death.*

* Such as desire to obtain further information on the

deep sufferings and memorable deliverances of Friends, more generally at that distressing period, will find them related in a small interesting volume, published in 1825, and entitled, "The Principles of Peace, Exemplified in the Conduct of the Society of Friends in Ireland, during the Rebellion of the year 1798." By Thomas Hancock, M. D. Tract No. 46, of the series published by the Tract Association of Friends, is, for the most part, an abridgment of the volume just referred to. It can be had at their Depository, No. 304 Arch Street, Philadelphia.

www.ingramcontent.com/pod-product-compliance
Lightning Source LLC
Chambersburg PA
CBHW021442090426
42739CB00009B/1596